THE RITUALS JOURNAL

Powerful
Practices
for Personal
Transformation

NATALIE MACNEIL

ILLUSTRATIONS BY LINDSAY HINE

CHRONICLE BOOKS
SAN FRANCISCO

ISBN 978-1-4521-8074-8

Manufactured in China.

Design by **Vanessa Dina** with **Kimberly Di Santo**.
Illustrations by **Lindsay Hine**.

10 9 8 7 6 5 4 3 2 1

Chronicle Books LLC
680 Second Street
San Francisco, CA 94107
www.chroniclebooks.com

J
O
U
R
N
A
L

Dear one,

I know you found your way to this journal for a reason. Maybe you're looking to discover your purpose or transform an area of your life, or maybe you want to incorporate rituals into your daily routine to stay centered and cultivate more joy. No matter what your reason is, where you are right now is a beautiful place to be. This is a moment of potential, choice, and expansive horizons opening before you. Everything has prepared you for this journey we're about to take together, a journey deep into your Self.

This journal combines rituals with a daily journaling practice. Rituals connect us to our needs and desires, to each other, to the earth, to other cultures, to our collective past and future, and to our curiosity around who we are and what we're doing here. Rituals are a concept as old as humanity, with the earliest known ritual dating back some seventy thousand years.

I believe journaling is one of the most transformative rituals you can commit to. It's a ritual some of the greatest thinkers, philosophers, inventors, and creatives have in common. Journaling reduces anxiety, improves emotional well-being, and increases happiness.

> *I'm curious if you ever feel a longing for something more in life or for the world to be different than it is right now?*

We are born into a world that is organized and translated for us, a world that tells us who we are and how we *should* be. We are taught how to sift and sort by labels, how to act so that others will love and accept us, and how to perceive what's around us and what everything we see means. That is, we learn what the meaning is to those who are guiding us. This guidance is, of course, useful and necessary for our early survival, but at the same time, in this learning process we're sold many lies that eclipse our innate wisdom and intuition.

Deep within and buried beneath layers of conditioning and shame and mistruths you have formed about yourself, your true Self—the truest version of who you are—beckons like a lighthouse guiding a boat safely and joyously to shore. That longing you feel is a call to come home to the real You. Rituals and journaling allow you to tap in to your true Self.

Have you ever stopped to think about how you would choose to see the world and be in the world if the world hadn't told you *who* you should be and *how* you should be? Many of us have been conditioned to seek our happiness, success, and fulfillment outside of ourselves. We search for something we think we'll find "someday" in a future that we believe isn't accessible right here and now. If you reflect on it though, you will realize this profound truth:

This moment, and what we are choosing in it, *is* our future.

As you move through this journal, you will begin to unlock your true Self. The practices in this experience will support you in traversing your inner world. They will guide you to a magnificent place where everything you have sought *out there* is awaiting your discovery; a place where you can powerfully create your future *now*.

These practices come from my journey of more than fifteen years of deep self-exploration. I've worked with incredible teachers around the world, trained in many modalities such as neurostrategic coaching and meditation, and committed to being a student of experiences that will be of the highest service on my path toward self-discovery. All of life is our teacher, every experience and every encounter giving us an opportunity to heal, to love, to forgive, to become more whole.

This daily journal ritual will help you let go of habits, behaviors, and thought patterns that are no longer serving you. And it will allow you to tap in to the oceans of wisdom within yourself, where you can discover a sense of aliveness and the power to manifest your deepest desires.

I'm inviting you to get real with yourself during this process. There are going to be parts of this experience that may make you uncomfortable. You might react with guilt, shame, or judgment. But remember that every difficult emotion that comes up is an invitation to love and accept yourself more fully and practice self-compassion.

I'm excited to hear what unfolds for you on this journey. Keep me updated @nataliemacneil on social media, and use the hashtag #theritualsjournal to chronicle and share.

One more gift for you: I've created supplemental materials to support and enhance your pilgrimage. You can visit discovertherituals.com for in-depth worksheets, guided audio meditations, and more practices.

> *May this experience open a portal of potentiality within you.*
>
> *May your path be blessed.*
>
> *May you remember who You are.*

HOW TO USE THIS JOURNAL

This journal is organized into two sections: The Core Rituals, starting on page 13, and The Daily Journal Ritual, starting on page 41.

SECTION ONE: **The Core Rituals**

In this section you'll find ten Core Rituals for you to dive into that are woven into Section Two. These practices invite you to get curious about how you live your life, and the future you want to create for yourself.

Each ritual in Section One begins with a "True North" note to illuminate where the practice leads you and what's possible if you use the ritual as a compass. I recommend doing one practice per day or a few a week. Giving yourself some space between each practice will allow you to process your discoveries so that you can integrate your learnings into every facet of your life.

SECTION TWO: **The Daily Journal Ritual**

In this section, you'll find prompts for a daily journaling practice that builds on the foundational practices introduced in Section One. The daily format is a tool for regular reflection and inquiry.

The morning begins with your Commitment of the Day. From there, you move into a list of the things you wish to embody. Finally, there's a Stream of Consciousness question to continue to explore your inner world, tune in to your intuition, and connect to your Higher Self. The evening starts with an Accountability Check-In on the commitment you made to the day. Then we move into a Flow of Gratitude practice, followed by exploring what the day revealed to you in a note to your future self.

I recommend keeping this journal on your nightstand and committing to a daily journaling ritual. Approach the practices with playfulness and curiosity, and find a journaling practice that works for you.

Now let's get started.

SECTION ONE

THE CORE RITUALS

YOUR
COMMITMENTS

———

TRUE NORTH: This ritual guides you to make commitments to your Self that will support you in getting the most out of this journaling practice, and also out of your life.

We make a lot of commitments to other people, but we rarely make commitments to ourselves. To begin this practice, I want to invite you to make two life-changing commitments:

Commitment #1: Compassionate Acceptance

Acceptance is part of the path of self-mastery, and it's a key to happiness and fulfillment. Acceptance isn't complacency, and it doesn't mean there won't be emotions and feelings that arise from things that have happened. It is simply acceptance of what can't be changed so you can free up your energy to focus on what *can* be changed, which is where we are heading next in this journey. You can't change how things have been up to this point. What you can do is accept it, and when you do, limitless future possibilities become available to you.

Say this phrase out loud:

I, _____, accept where I am right now, and all that has happened up to this point. I commit to focusing on what I have the power to change now.

Commitment #2: Radical Personal Responsibility

At the heart of being able to change areas of your life and create what you really want is radical personal responsibility. It's not always easy. For many, the default is to shift blame outside ourselves, deflect, and avoid. This strategy might make it feel easier to deal with difficult situations, but it is disempowering in ways you may not yet realize. Every time you choose not to take ownership for your role, you are telling yourself that you do not have sovereignty and power over your own life. And that is a lie—perhaps one of the biggest lies we tell ourselves.

Say this phrase out loud:

I, _____, am committed to radical personal responsibility from this point forward in my life.

SKY
GAZING

———

TRUE NORTH: This ritual guides you to gently observe your present thoughts and feelings.

This concept is inspired by the Tibetan Buddhist practice of gazing at the sky. Your true nature is like the sky's vast blue, and thoughts and feelings and beliefs are like weather systems and clouds—none of which *are* the sky. The sky remains neutral and does not get attached to—nor does it identify with—the clouds that come and go.

We all experience feelings of frustration, uncertainty, and fear from time to time. Our personal work is to not identify *as* those feelings and to instead see them like clouds that pass through the vast blue sky of our true, divine, and luminous nature.

You are not your thoughts or emotions, although it can certainly feel that way at times. You can think a thought, you can feel an emotion, you can believe a belief. But you are not those things. I invite you to consider:

Who is the thinker? Who is the feeler? Who is the one believing?

Contemplating those questions can deepen your relationship with your Self, reveal your purpose, and bring more peace and clarity to your life.

To begin your journey of self-exploration, I invite you to spend some time sky gazing as you contemplate this concept. Notice what clouds pass across your sky, and observe them without attachment or judgment. Return to this practice whenever you feel overwhelmed by lots of thoughts, emotions, or stresses and need to find some clarity and calm.

MINDFUL
MORNING

―――――

TRUTH NORTH: This ritual helps you start your day powerfully and mindfully, feeling grounded.

Morning rituals and routines can set the tone for your entire day. I like to spend a few moments each morning visualizing myself in the eye of a hurricane, calm though things around me are chaotic. It centers me before I jump into my day. I will often do a breathing ritual, too, taking long and loud breaths, and rooting myself deep into the earth with each breath. This practice makes me feel I can withstand anything that may come my way.

Having an anchoring morning ritual will help you begin each day equipped and grounded so that you can handle anything that comes your way. Even when you're confronted with difficulties, you will be able to face the situation with everything you've got and make the best decision for yourself in the moment.

So consider: When you wake up in the morning, how are you starting your day? Are you jumping right into the hurricane? Are you automatically reaching for your phone or computer to review the news and to-do lists and emails? Or are you taking the time to make sure that you are planted in the calm eye of the storm so that you know that you can handle anything that comes your way?

There is no one-size-fits-all morning ritual, and your individual circumstances determine how much time you have before you need to do things like drive to work or get the kids ready for school. You can't take on someone else's routine and hope that it will work exactly the same for you.

Your morning ritual is yours to design. There's just one thing: Now that you have this journal, I recommend reaching for it first thing in the morning instead of your phone and taking a couple minutes to do The Daily Journal Ritual (page 41).

Here are a few things to keep in mind as you design your own morning ritual:

Hold off on checking your phone first thing in the morning. That immediately takes you out of the calm center of the hurricane. Our phones are amazing tools, but they also drown us in information and must-dos without pause. It's a good idea to set your phone on airplane mode as you go to bed and return it to normal only after your morning ritual is done. Try it!

Hydrate. After not having water for several hours, your body needs it first thing in the morning to boost your metabolism and flush toxins. Keep a big glass of water by your bedside to drink upon waking.

Do something for your body, something for your mind, and something for your spirit. Our bodies need to move, and moving first thing in the morning creates movement and momentum for the day ahead. Put on a song you love and dance, stretch, do squats and push-ups, or do any combination of the above. Spend a few minutes meditating and breathing deeply to start the day with a calm mind. Close your eyes and think of five things you're thankful for. You can do this with loved ones, too, and build a ritual together.

Now you're ready to start your day.

FLOW
OF
GRATITUDE

TRUE NORTH: This ritual guides you to appreciate all the blessings in your life, expand your capacity for joy, and invest in the future life you want to be living.

Look around you. Can you see in front of you some dreams that you once dreamed? There's a lot to be grateful for. Giving thanks is a common practice in most cultures. "Thank you" and "You're welcome" are staples of polite, everyday conversation. But do we really *feel* the high of gratitude and experience the power of it when we say a quick "Thanks" to someone? And, how often are we cultivating gratitude toward ourselves?

For this practice, set a timer for three minutes and express everything you're grateful for and feel positive about in your life, until the timer is up. Keep going for the whole three minutes. If you feel stuck or something isn't coming to you, take a few deep breaths and feel gratitude for being alive and breathing in this moment, then get back into the flow.

Consider the areas of your life you are most happy with, the positive feelings you're experiencing and what evokes them, what you're proud of yourself for, who you appreciate and why, the small things that bring you joy, the beauty you've created in your life and how you contribute to the lives of others and to the world.

Ready? Go!

I invite you to make gratitude a daily practice and have fun with it. You can do Flow of Gratitude next time you're stopped at a red light or crosswalk, out loud with your loved ones when sharing a meal, or anytime and anywhere when you want to boost your mood.

Review what you wrote in this practice, and celebrate all that is good. Dwell in that space. What you focus on, you get more of. Eckhart Tolle says, "Gratitude for the present moment and the fullness of life is the true prosperity." A prosperous and abundant life is available to you here and now. Claim it with your gratitude.

THE
BEAUTY
OF
WHAT
IS

TRUE NORTH: This ritual will help you deepen your self-love and acceptance (for your partner, friends, family, and yourself).

We are all perfectly imperfect. Accepting that fact about ourselves and others is liberating and can save a lot of energy we expend when we want something or someone to be different than it is right now. This ritual invites you to see beauty in imperfection and deliberately seek out reasons to embrace and adore yourself and those around you.

This practice is embodied in the Japanese tradition of *wabi-sabi*. While there's no direct translation from Japanese to English, essentially it refers to the practice of appreciating authenticity over perfection. It's the belief that there's beauty in a chipped vase, a cloudy December landscape, aged wood, or a rusted piece of metal. It's the practice of looking at something that seems, at first, dismissible or unwanted and finding its beauty.

When it comes to your relationship with yourself and others, can you open up to seeing flaws as expressions of our existence as human beings? Recognizing this, and practicing how to appreciate authenticity, can open new doors for connection, appreciation, and love.

When someone close to you does something that doesn't meet an expectation you had or triggers you, take a moment before you react and ask yourself, "Is reacting to this worth my time and energy right now? Based on past experiences, what will happen after I react and how will I feel?" Before you react, find three things you love and appreciate about that person— three things about them that make you happy—and hold these in your mind as you take a few breaths. Extend this love to them in your heart, and then choose how you want to respond.

Yes, it's easier said than done. This isn't about being perfect; remember, it's called a "practice" for a reason. Practice.

To do this practice with yourself, begin by standing in front of a mirror. What do you see? Hold yourself authentically; don't pose. You are witnessing the beauty of your own being.

Look into your own eyes and hold your gaze. Focus on breathing deeply. After you've taken eight deep inhalations and exhalations, take your gaze to the rest of your body.

Express love and gratitude for yourself and where you're at in your journey right now. What's something you're proud of? What's something small you can acknowledge yourself for? As you look at this beautiful reflection, pause on any area you have struggled to accept sometimes. Now, instead of judging what you see, say something loving to that part of yourself.

Finish this practice by giving yourself a compliment the way you would give a compliment to someone you really love and care about. Practice this ritual daily and watch your relationship with yourself and others transform before your eyes.

BREATHE

IT

OUT

TRUTH NORTH: This ritual is ideal for releasing stress, connecting to your body, and developing mindfulness.

Your body breathes, on its own, without any conscious instruction on your part. Your lungs expand and contract with the flow of air, delivering oxygen to your cells, brain, organs, and every part of your body. Take a moment to appreciate your remarkable respiratory system before you dive into this ritual.

It's been proven that mindful breathing, when practiced every day, has enormous benefits, including reducing anxiety, preventing heart disease, improving mental and physical performance, clearing and opening your chakras, and boosting your mood. Ancient yogic breath-work techniques called *pranayama* have been tapping in to these benefits for centuries.

Too many of us feel as though we have to wait for our next yoga class, massage, or night alone at home in order to really relax and unwind. That's simply not true. This is a ritual you can do anytime, anywhere. All you need is a timer, somewhere comfortable to sit or stand, and a little music (if you wish). You can even set an alarm for a random time during the day that says "Breathe It Out" so you're reminded to take a few minutes to recenter.

Let's begin.

Set a timer (with a peaceful alarm tone) for three minutes. If you'd like to play some calming music, put that on.

In a standing or seated position, breathe in deeply for a count of four seconds, and then breathe out deeply for a count of four seconds.

Feel your feet on the floor and your spine in alignment, and relax.

With every inhalation, feel the breath in your body, and with every exhalation, let go of stress and tension in your body.

If visualizations feel supportive to you in this process, here are two visualizations you can try:

1. On your inhalation, visualize the core of a ball of light in your heart, and on your exhalation, see that ball of light expanding and filling your heart. This visualization will support you when your heart feels tender, heavy, or closed.

2. On your inhalation, visualize light pouring through the top of your head, and on your exhalation, move that light down your body and out the bottoms of your feet. Every time you exhale, imagine roots growing downward from your feet, grounding you deep into the earth and her soul. This visualization will ground you and make you feel strong and ready for anything that comes your way.

When the timer goes off, you'll feel renewed inside and out, ready to face the rest of the day.

To download a guided breathwork practice, visit discovertherituals.com.

ENCHANTED
EVENING

In many cultures around the world, sleep is sacred. Our system has evolved to follow a pattern, the circadian rhythm, that directs when to be active and when to rest. But many of us face the temptation to keep working and being productive into the night, which ultimately disrupts our natural rhythms and exhausts our bodies.

Resting properly is crucial for restoring your brain connections, allowing memories to become fixed, as well as for maintaining your overall health and productivity. Sometimes sleep can help you get more done than doing more work can, as counterintuitive as that may seem.

In this ritual, you're invited to create an evening practice for yourself that feels nourishing and prepares your body for rest.

Here are a few things to get you started in designing your evening ritual:

Remove blue light from your environment at least two hours before bed. Blue light from your computer and phone screens suppresses melatonin production.

Your phone likely has a setting for night mode, where blue light is removed from the screen after the sun goes down, and you can download a computer app that will remove the blue light from your computer screen in the evening too.

Clear your mind. As you start to wind down for the evening, you probably still have things from the day running through your mind. Therapeutic journaling is an effective way to let them go, and you're one step ahead by owning this journal. End your day by filling out the evening practice from The Daily Journal Ritual (page 41).

Connect with loved ones. Root yourself in what matters most, whether that's time at home with your family or calling someone to catch up. There is nothing more important than the people we get to share our lives with.

Clean off the day. Further release tension with a cleansing shower or bath. Visualize the water washing away the day to prepare you fully for rest.

Put your phone on airplane mode. Do this before climbing into bed. A transmitting phone next to you at night may affect your sleep. Sweet dreams, dear one.

A
VISIT
WITH
YOUR
FUTURE
SELF

TRUE NORTH: This ritual will guide you to reimagine the life you want to be living, and get clarity on what you truly want.

In this ritual, you are going to time travel and sit down for a visit with your future self. You can choose to focus on any future time you wish—a month from now, a year from now, a decade from now, or beyond—and you can use this practice to visit your future self at many different ages and stages in your life.

I recommend setting aside 15 to 20 minutes as you don't want to rush through this important visit. Imagine the two of you sitting in a living room, on a beach, in a café, or at another favorite spot. Picture as many vivid details as you can, and try to include all five senses. Think about the temperature, the light, what you can see, hear, and smell, and the way your body feels.

Ask your future self questions, and allow them to ask you questions, too. Here are some questions you may want to ask:

Who are you at this time in your life?

Who are the people that surround you?

How do you spend your time?

What are you proud of?

What are some of your best memories?

What positive contribution are you making?

Who are you making that contribution for?

What did you learn about yourself on the journey to this place?

If you could go back in time, would you do anything differently?

What's important for me to know?

Share your wisdom, your fears, and your hopes. When you're done, you can write down the highlights of your visit if you feel inspired to.

For a guided audio of this practice, visit discovertherituals.com.

EMBODY
YOUR
FUTURE
NOW

TRUE NORTH: This ritual will guide you to embody your deepest truth and most heartfelt desires, and express yourself more fully.

This is a ritual for manifesting what you want most. The secret to having everything you desire is *being* that which you desire now, in this moment. You can bring to life any vision that you become the embodiment of.

In this practice, you'll be choosing words that capture the essence of your vision for your future. I call these the Essences of Embodiment. I've created a list of essences you can choose from, but I invite you to find your own words that you connect deeply with.

Start by tuning in to your dream future (I recommend doing A Visit with Your Future Self on page 31

as preparation, before you dive in to this practice).
What do you see for your relationships, health, career,
finances, personal growth, and whatever else is
important to you? What is the quality, or the essence,
of that way of being you see in your future vision? For
example, let's say you really want to build a successful
business around your creative passions. What are the
characteristics—what I call Essences of Embodiment—
that will help you achieve that vision? The essences of
leadership, organization, and abundance may feel true.

Here are some Essences of Embodiment to explore, and
I invite you to choose a few that feel in alignment with
your vision:

Abundance	Divinity
Adventure	Ecstasy
Alignment	Empowerment
Aliveness	Expansion
Artistry	Femininity
Beauty	Fire
Bravery	Forward motion
Connection	Freedom
Courage	Fulfillment
Creativity	Generosity
Divine Mother	Grace

Gratitude	Possibility
Hustle	Power
Imagination	Presence
Impact	Radiance
Innovation	Receptivity
Inspiration	Self-expression
Intimacy	Sensuality
Knowing	Service
Leadership	Sexuality
Liberation	Simplicity
Love	Strength
Luxury	Truth
Magic	Visibility
Magnetism	Wanderlust
Organization	Wealth
Overflow	Wellness
Passion	Wonder
Playfulness	Worthiness

Now it's time to embody these essences to create your future right here in this moment. Don't just think about being more of the essence you have chosen. That's more in the mind, and in this practice I invite you to take these essences into your five senses and into your body. *Be* the essence, almost as if it's a person. See the difference?

Consider:

How does this essence feel?

How does this essence speak?

What does this essence hear?

How does this essence walk?

How does this essence show up to work?

What does this essence love to do?

For example, if the essence you're embodying is "possibility," possibility may feel totally unstoppable, walk into a meeting and speak powerfully without holding back its brilliance, and hear opportunities in the situations that may bring up fear for other people. Possibility may take bigger risks, and aim for bolder goals.

Like all the practices in this book, get curious and playful with it. You can choose essences for different areas of your life or different goals. You can choose different essences each day, and you can even choose essences for a specific situation like a date you're going on or an important meeting you have.

To dive deeper into this practice, go to discovertherituals.com.

STREAM
OF
CONSCIOUSNESS

TRUE NORTH: This ritual will guide you in developing your intuition and trusting the wisdom within you.

Writing can heal, cleanse, liberate. Stream of consciousness writing is a technique to free the mind of its normal restrictions, cleansing it to transmit intuitive messages from the deepest wells of wisdom that are within you.

In this stream of consciousness practice, you simply put pen to paper and write words as they go through your mind. Don't try to make everything make sense. Instead, allow for "mistakes" and "nonsense." Connect to the source of your thoughts and observe them in your writing without passing judgment. In the Daily Journal Section (page 41), there is an opportunity for you to develop this practice of listening to your inner wisdom every morning.

To open yourself to this ritual, we'll begin with a simple question:

What does my inner wisdom want me to know right now?

Spend at least five minutes meditating on this question. Sit comfortably, close your eyes, and focus on your belly and your chest expanding and contracting with your breath. If you like using imagery, you can visualize a bright light coming in through the top of your head as you inhale and spreading to envelop your body as you exhale. Be present with your intention.

When you feel ready and in the flow, open your eyes and start writing everything that comes into your mind. Allow yourself to be free! Continue writing the flow of your thoughts until you've put everything onto paper.

If you wish, you can return to your stream of consciousness writing and start unraveling the meaning behind it. It's also okay to not reread the writing and instead stay with the meaning you found in the experience of writing. Either way, automatic stream of consciousness writing will be an illuminating tool on your path to connecting with yourself and expanding your intuition in new ways.

THE DAILY
JOURNAL
RITUAL

THE DAILY JOURNAL RITUAL OVERVIEW

You're invited to continue this journey with a simple daily journaling ritual that incorporates some of the rituals introduced in Section One. The daily format is a tool for reflection, inquiry, and tuning in to your intuition. It's a place to embody your future now.

MORNING JOURNALING

Today I Am Committed To:
Make a clear commitment to the day ahead.

Today I Am Embodying the Essences Of:
What essences will you embody today that align with your highest intention? Pick three words that capture the way you want to feel today.

Stream of Consciousness
Finally, there's a Stream of Consciousness question to help you explore your inner world and tune in to your intuition. Relinquish control and remove any filters so that you can listen to the true wisdom of your Self. Simply put pen to paper and write words as they go through your mind. This is a lovely way to connect to your inner wisdom each day so that you can make decisions aligned with your Self and purpose.

EVENING JOURNALING

Accountability Check-In
The Evening Journaling page starts with a check-in on the
commitment you made to the day.

Flow of Gratitude
Move into a short Flow of Gratitude practice. This practice
guides you to appreciate all the blessings in your life, expand
your capacity for joy, and invest in the future life you want to
be living. Close your eyes and consider the areas of your life
you are most happy with, the beauty you've created in your
life, and how you contribute to the lives of others and to the
world. Then spend a few minutes writing about the things
you feel grateful for today, big or small. A prosperous and
abundant life is available to you here and now. Claim it with
your gratitude.

What Did Today Reveal to Me?
In this section of the evening practice, you're asked the question, "What did today reveal to me?" Life is always speaking
to you and revealing new things, and this is an opportunity to
reflect on any ideas that came to you, memorable moments,
signs from the Universe, lessons learned, etc.

Dear Future Me
End with a note to your future self. How can your future self
implement what you learned and experienced today for a
more fulfilled, joyous, and realized life?

Below, you'll find an example of the Daily Journal practice.

MORNING JOURNALING EXAMPLE

Today I am committed to:
Staying focused on my project and not allowing anything to distract me from making inspired progress toward completing it.

Today I am embodying the essences of:
Knowing, divine creativity, and contribution.

Stream of consciousness
Today's question: *What am I currently choosing not to see that would expand my Self if I could see it?*

I am choosing not to see that taking on less work and lightening the load I have been carrying will not mean I will have less, be less, or be settling for less. How many times have I heard the phrase "Less is more" and rolled my eyes? But there is truth in that. There is beauty in the simple path ahead of me. By taking on less I have a far greater capacity and would impact more people.

EVENING JOURNALING EXAMPLE

I followed through on the commitment I made.

Flow of gratitude
I'm grateful for my Beloved, our connection, and the support I'm feeling from him as I finish writing this book. I'm grateful for the focus group I hosted today going through the core rituals from this journal. I feel so blessed to get to do the work I do in the world. I'm grateful for the city of Los Angeles, which brought me so much joy today as I walked around and connected with people and art and the ocean. I'm grateful for the man who made up a song about me in Venice today, and the beauty of connection and presence with people. I'm grateful to feel in love with all of life and to feel all of life in love with me.

What did today reveal to me?
Today revealed how amazing it feels to start the morning in a calm and grounded place with the Breathe It Out ritual. I am committed to continuing the practice!

While I was in a meeting today I had a memory of being a child and holding back on sharing in class, mostly because I cared so much about what others thought of me and I got teased for being smart. Every time I felt an impulse to contribute to the discussion or answer a question and I didn't, I felt a tension. Today in an important meeting, I was holding back a bit and I felt that same tension I remember from childhood. Reflecting more deeply on the situation today and what it would look like for me to fully express myself, I am challenging myself to share, contribute, and express myself fully for the next week and see how that feels. I'm grateful for the awareness I'm developing in so many areas of my life right now.

Dear future me,

Express yourself fully in that next meeting. Your voice and your perspective matter.

Did you journal today? Awesome, keep it up.

I love you ;)

Oh and remember to call your parents!

MORNING

DATE:

Today I am committed to:

_____

Today I am embodying the essences of:

_____

STREAM OF CONSCIOUSNESS
Today's question: *What am I avoiding? If I chose to confront it, what would be possible?*

_____

_____

_____

_____

_____

_____

_____

_____

_____

EVENING

I FOLLOWED THROUGH ON THE COMMITMENT I MADE. ☐

Flow of gratitude

What did today reveal to me?

Dear future me,

MORNING

DATE:

Today I am committed to:

Today I am embodying the essences of:

STREAM OF CONSCIOUSNESS

Today's question: *Where am I currently settling for "good enough"? What would be available to me if I was no longer willing to settle?*

EVENING

I FOLLOWED THROUGH ON THE COMMITMENT I MADE. ☐

Flow of gratitude

What did today reveal to me?

Dear future me,

MORNING

DATE:

Today I am committed to:

_____

Today I am embodying the essences of:

_____

STREAM OF CONSCIOUSNESS
Today's question: *What do I love about my life?*

_____

_____

_____

_____

_____

_____

_____

_____

_____

_____

EVENING

I FOLLOWED THROUGH ON THE COMMITMENT I MADE. ☐

Flow of gratitude

_____

_____

_____

_____

_____

What did today reveal to me?

_____

_____

_____

_____

_____

Dear future me,

_____

_____

_____

MORNING

DATE:

Today I am committed to:

Today I am embodying the essences of:

STREAM OF CONSCIOUSNESS
Today's question: *What is my heart yearning for?*

EVENING

I FOLLOWED THROUGH ON THE COMMITMENT I MADE. ☐

Flow of gratitude

What did today reveal to me?

Dear future me,

MORNING

DATE:

Today I am committed to:

_____

Today I am embodying the essences of:

_____

STREAM OF CONSCIOUSNESS

Today's question: *What am I most afraid of? What future possibilities are available to me when I face off with that fear?*

_____

_____

_____

_____

_____

_____

_____

_____

_____

EVENING

I FOLLOWED THROUGH ON THE COMMITMENT I MADE. ☐

Flow of gratitude

_____

_____

_____

_____

_____

_____

What did today reveal to me?

_____

_____

_____

_____

_____

Dear future me,

_____

_____

_____

MORNING

DATE:

Today I am committed to:

_____

Today I am embodying the essences of:

_____

STREAM OF CONSCIOUSNESS
Today's question: *What can I upgrade and set higher standards
for in my life?*

_____

_____

_____

_____

_____

_____

_____

_____

_____

_____

EVENING

I FOLLOWED THROUGH ON THE COMMITMENT I MADE. ☐

Flow of gratitude

_____

_____

_____

_____

_____

What did today reveal to me?

_____

_____

_____

_____

_____

Dear future me,

_____

_____

_____

MORNING

DATE:

Today I am committed to:

Today I am embodying the essences of:

STREAM OF CONSCIOUSNESS
Today's question: *How would I show up differently in my life if I stopped trying to manage how other people experience me?*

EVENING

I FOLLOWED THROUGH ON THE COMMITMENT I MADE. ☐

Flow of gratitude

What did today reveal to me?

Dear future me,

MORNING

DATE:

Today I am committed to:

_____

Today I am embodying the essences of:

_____

Today's question: *What are the values that act as a compass for everything I do and for my way of being?*

_____

_____

_____

_____

_____

_____

_____

_____

_____

_____

EVENING

I FOLLOWED THROUGH ON THE COMMITMENT I MADE. ☐

Flow of gratitude

_____

_____

_____

_____

_____

What did today reveal to me?

_____

_____

_____

_____

_____

Dear future me,

_____

_____

_____

MORNING

DATE:

Today I am committed to:

Today I am embodying the essences of:

STREAM OF CONSCIOUSNESS
Today's question: *What am I here to do?*

EVENING

I FOLLOWED THROUGH ON THE COMMITMENT I MADE. ☐

Flow of gratitude

What did today reveal to me?

Dear future me,

MORNING

DATE:

Today I am committed to:

_____

Today I am embodying the essences of:

_____

STREAM OF CONSCIOUSNESS
Today's question: *If money wasn't a factor, how would I choose to live?*

_____

_____

_____

_____

_____

_____

_____

_____

_____

EVENING

I FOLLOWED THROUGH ON THE COMMITMENT I MADE. ☐

Flow of gratitude

_____

_____

_____

_____

_____

What did today reveal to me?

_____

_____

_____

_____

_____

Dear future me,

_____

_____

_____

MORNING

DATE:

Today I am committed to:

_____

Today I am embodying the essences of:

_____

STREAM OF CONSCIOUSNESS

Today's question: *What strengths do I have that others see in me, but that I have not fully owned within myself?*

_____

_____

_____

_____

_____

_____

_____

_____

_____

EVENING

I FOLLOWED THROUGH ON THE COMMITMENT I MADE. ☐

Flow of gratitude

What did today reveal to me?

Dear future me,

MORNING

DATE:

Today I am committed to:

_____

Today I am embodying the essences of:

_____

STREAM OF CONSCIOUSNESS
Today's question: *What behaviors, patterns, beliefs, and thoughts do I have that aren't serving my highest path forward?*

_____

_____

_____

_____

_____

_____

_____

_____

_____

EVENING

I FOLLOWED THROUGH ON THE COMMITMENT I MADE. ☐

Flow of gratitude

_____

_____

_____

_____

_____

_____

What did today reveal to me?

_____

_____

_____

_____

_____

Dear future me,

_____

_____

_____

MORNING

DATE:

Today I am committed to:

_____

Today I am embodying the essences of:

_____

STREAM OF CONSCIOUSNESS
Today's question: *What exists in the world because of me?*

_____

_____

_____

_____

_____

_____

_____

_____

_____

_____

EVENING

I FOLLOWED THROUGH ON THE COMMITMENT I MADE. ☐

Flow of gratitude

What did today reveal to me?

Dear future me,

MORNING

DATE:

Today I am committed to:

_____

Today I am embodying the essences of:

_____

STREAM OF CONSCIOUSNESS

Today's question: *Who are my biggest supporters? How can I show them appreciation today?*

_____

_____

_____

_____

_____

_____

_____

_____

_____

_____

EVENING

I FOLLOWED THROUGH ON THE COMMITMENT I MADE. ☐

Flow of gratitude

_____

_____

_____

_____

_____

_____

What did today reveal to me?

_____

_____

_____

_____

_____

Dear future me,

_____

_____

_____

MORNING

DATE:

Today I am committed to:

_____

Today I am embodying the essences of:

_____

STREAM OF CONSCIOUSNESS
Today's question: *Who would I love to attract into my life?*
Who do I have to be to attract this person?

_____

_____

_____

_____

_____

_____

_____

_____

EVENING

I FOLLOWED THROUGH ON THE COMMITMENT I MADE. ☐

Flow of gratitude

What did today reveal to me?

Dear future me,

MORNING

DATE:

Today I am committed to:

_____

Today I am embodying the essences of:

_____

STREAM OF CONSCIOUSNESS
Today's question: *Where would more boundaries serve me in my relationships?*

_____

_____

_____

_____

_____

_____

_____

_____

_____

_____

EVENING

I FOLLOWED THROUGH ON THE COMMITMENT I MADE. ☐

Flow of gratitude

What did today reveal to me?

Dear future me,

MORNING

DATE:

Today I am committed to:

Today I am embodying the essences of:

STREAM OF CONSCIOUSNESS
Today's question: *What obstacles am I most proud of overcoming to get to where I am right now?*

EVENING

I FOLLOWED THROUGH ON THE COMMITMENT I MADE. ☐

Flow of gratitude

What did today reveal to me?

Dear future me,

MORNING

DATE:

Today I am committed to:

_____

Today I am embodying the essences of:

_____

STREAM OF CONSCIOUSNESS
Today's question: *How can I experience more pleasure?*

_____

_____

_____

_____

_____

_____

_____

_____

_____

_____

EVENING

I FOLLOWED THROUGH ON THE COMMITMENT I MADE. ☐

Flow of gratitude

What did today reveal to me?

Dear future me,

MORNING

DATE:

Today I am committed to:

Today I am embodying the essences of:

STREAM OF CONSCIOUSNESS
Today's question: *What lessons have I gleaned from painful experiences?*

EVENING

I FOLLOWED THROUGH ON THE COMMITMENT I MADE. ☐

Flow of gratitude

What did today reveal to me?

Dear future me,

MORNING

DATE:

Today I am committed to:

Today I am embodying the essences of:

STREAM OF CONSCIOUSNESS
Today's question: *What "mistake" am I most grateful for having made?*

EVENING

I FOLLOWED THROUGH ON THE COMMITMENT I MADE. ☐

Flow of gratitude

_____

_____

_____

_____

_____

What did today reveal to me?

_____

_____

_____

_____

_____

Dear future me,

_____

_____

_____

MORNING

DATE:

Today I am committed to:

_____

Today I am embodying the essences of:

_____

STREAM OF CONSCIOUSNESS
Today's question: *What haven't I celebrated in my life that deserves celebration?*

_____

_____

_____

_____

_____

_____

_____

_____

EVENING

I FOLLOWED THROUGH ON THE COMMITMENT I MADE. ☐

Flow of gratitude

_____

_____

_____

_____

_____

What did today reveal to me?

_____

_____

_____

_____

_____

Dear future me,

_____

_____

_____

MORNING

DATE:

Today I am committed to:

_____

Today I am embodying the essences of:

_____

STREAM OF CONSCIOUSNESS
Today's question: *What would I like to forgive others for?*

_____

_____

_____

_____

_____

_____

_____

_____

_____

_____

_____

EVENING

I FOLLOWED THROUGH ON THE COMMITMENT I MADE. ☐

Flow of gratitude

What did today reveal to me?

Dear future me,

MORNING

DATE:

Today I am committed to:

Today I am embodying the essences of:

STREAM OF CONSCIOUSNESS
Today's question: *What would I like to forgive myself for?*

EVENING

I FOLLOWED THROUGH ON THE COMMITMENT I MADE. ☐

Flow of gratitude

What did today reveal to me?

Dear future me,

MORNING

DATE:

Today I am committed to:

Today I am embodying the essences of:

STREAM OF CONSCIOUSNESS
Today's question: *In what situations and relationships do I feel most powerful?*

EVENING

I FOLLOWED THROUGH ON THE COMMITMENT I MADE. ☐

Flow of gratitude

_____

_____

_____

_____

_____

What did today reveal to me?

_____

_____

_____

_____

_____

Dear future me,

_____

_____

_____

MORNING

DATE:

Today I am committed to:

Today I am embodying the essences of:

STREAM OF CONSCIOUSNESS
Today's question: *In what situations am I giving away my power?*

EVENING

I FOLLOWED THROUGH ON THE COMMITMENT I MADE. ☐

Flow of gratitude

What did today reveal to me?

Dear future me,

MORNING

DATE:

Today I am committed to:

Today I am embodying the essences of:

STREAM OF CONSCIOUSNESS
Today's question: *What is draining my energy right now?*

EVENING

I FOLLOWED THROUGH ON THE COMMITMENT I MADE. ☐

Flow of gratitude

What did today reveal to me?

Dear future me,

MORNING

DATE:

Today I am committed to:

_____

Today I am embodying the essences of:

_____

STREAM OF CONSCIOUSNESS
Today's question: *What can I simplify and how?*

_____

_____

_____

_____

_____

_____

_____

_____

_____

_____

EVENING

I FOLLOWED THROUGH ON THE COMMITMENT I MADE. ☐

Flow of gratitude

_____

_____

_____

_____

_____

What did today reveal to me?

_____

_____

_____

_____

_____

Dear future me,

_____

_____

_____

MORNING

DATE:

Today I am committed to:

_____

Today I am embodying the essences of:

_____

STREAM OF CONSCIOUSNESS
Today's question: *What was my favorite activity to do as a child and how did it make me feel? What can I do today to embody that feeling?*

_____

_____

_____

_____

_____

_____

_____

_____

_____

EVENING

I FOLLOWED THROUGH ON THE COMMITMENT I MADE. ☐

Flow of gratitude

What did today reveal to me?

Dear future me,

MORNING

DATE:

Today I am committed to:

_____

Today I am embodying the essences of:

_____

STREAM OF CONSCIOUSNESS
Today's question: *What is something I can do now that will matter a year from now?*

_____

_____

_____

_____

_____

_____

_____

_____

_____

EVENING

I FOLLOWED THROUGH ON THE COMMITMENT I MADE. ☐

Flow of gratitude

_____

_____

_____

_____

What did today reveal to me?

_____

_____

_____

_____

Dear future me,

_____

_____

_____

MORNING

DATE:

Today I am committed to:

_____

Today I am embodying the essences of:

_____

STREAM OF CONSCIOUSNESS

Today's question: _What is a supportive decision I can make for myself right now? What have I been waiting for to make that decision?_

_____

_____

_____

_____

_____

_____

_____

_____

_____

EVENING

I FOLLOWED THROUGH ON THE COMMITMENT I MADE. ☐

Flow of gratitude

_____

_____

_____

_____

_____

_____

What did today reveal to me?

_____

_____

_____

_____

_____

_____

Dear future me,

_____

_____

_____

MORNING

DATE:

Today I am committed to:

_____

Today I am embodying the essences of:

_____

STREAM OF CONSCIOUSNESS
Today's question: *If my only job was to be happy, what would my day look like?*

_____

_____

_____

_____

_____

_____

_____

_____

EVENING

I FOLLOWED THROUGH ON THE COMMITMENT I MADE. ☐

Flow of gratitude

What did today reveal to me?

Dear future me,

MORNING

DATE:

Today I am committed to:

Today I am embodying the essences of:

STREAM OF CONSCIOUSNESS

Today's question: *What turns on my creativity?*

EVENING

I FOLLOWED THROUGH ON THE COMMITMENT I MADE. ☐

Flow of gratitude

_____

_____

_____

_____

_____

_____

What did today reveal to me?

_____

_____

_____

_____

_____

Dear future me,

_____

_____

_____

MORNING

DATE:

Today I am committed to:

Today I am embodying the essences of:

STREAM OF CONSCIOUSNESS

Today's question: *What secret am I harboring that would feel good to share and release? Who can I trust it with?*

EVENING

I FOLLOWED THROUGH ON THE COMMITMENT I MADE. ☐

Flow of gratitude

What did today reveal to me?

Dear future me,

MORNING

DATE:

Today I am committed to:

_____

Today I am embodying the essences of:

_____

STREAM OF CONSCIOUSNESS

Today's question: *What is something I have been afraid of expressing to someone? What might open up in that relationship if I have the courage to share it?*

_____

_____

_____

_____

_____

_____

_____

_____

_____

EVENING

I FOLLOWED THROUGH ON THE COMMITMENT I MADE. ☐

Flow of gratitude

_____

_____

_____

_____

_____

_____

What did today reveal to me?

_____

_____

_____

_____

_____

Dear future me,

_____

_____

_____

What a journey we have been on together. I invite you to close your eyes and think back to when you first opened this journal, then answer the questions below about your experience with this practice.

> *What have you remembered about Yourself along the way?*

> *What have you transformed in your life through The Daily Journal Ritual?*

> *What lessons have you learned, and how have you been embodying this wisdom?*

> *What are you loving about your life right now?*

> *Anything else you want to note about this journey?*

I would love for you to share your reflections with me. You can find me on Instagram using the handle @nataliemacneil.

Want to dive deeper into You?
Visit discovertherituals.com to . . .

Download additional resources and worksheets

Access guided audio practices

*Sign up for a digital coaching experience with me
to do this work in a more personalized way and be
guided to your next best steps*

It has been a joy sharing this practice with you.

—*Natalie*

I am so grateful for my Love, Yossef. He's been such an amazing support and sounding board as I've created this book and pored over every practice. He was also instrumental in the editing process, and I'm deeply grateful to him for that and for a million other things. I am grateful for the amazing focus group I had for this book so I could test each practice. Twanna Toliver, Sheila Devi, Tamar Hermes, Angela Somwaiya, Adriana Dunaev, Tamara Von Dohren, Tressa Beheim, and Andrea A. Noel really helped me refine it and get it to the finish line. I believe it is important to honor our teachers, and I am eternally grateful for mine. You have influenced the work I share with the world, and I will forever send blessings your way: Steve Linder, Byron Katie, Adyashanti, Richard Rudd, A Course in Miracles, Harville Hendrix, and all the others I've learned from in my self-discovery journey. I'm grateful for my dear friend Alyssa Nobriga who leaves me in awe with her insights and just lit me up when I talked to her on the phone a few minutes ago. I'm grateful for Layla Martin and all the magic our deep friendship creates and spills out into the world. I'm grateful for my loving and hilarious and supportive family who I love and adore. I'm grateful for my LA community that I don't have space to list individually, but I loooove you all. And I'm grateful for my agent Mel Flashman; the publisher of this book and *The Rituals*, Chronicle Books; and my editor, Rachel Hiles. Because of them, my divine creative inspiration gets channeled into books that make their way around the world. What a beautiful life. Always and forever grateful.

F
L
O
W

O
F

G
R
A
T
I
T
U
D
E

NATALIE MACNEIL is an Emmy Award–winning media entrepreneur listed on the Levo 100 as a "transformer of our generation" and featured by *Inc.* as one of "27 Women Leaders Changing the World." She is devoted to expanding human potential and inspiring people to live deeply meaningful lives through her books, videos, coaching experiences, and live events. She has been featured in *Elle*, *Glamour*, *People*, *TIME*, *Forbes*, *Inc.*, *Entrepreneur*, and more.

CONNECT WITH NATALIE:
Website: nataliemacneil.com
Instagram: @nataliemacneil
Facebook: /nataliemacneil
YouTube: /NatalieMacNeilTV

Chronicle Books publishes distinctive books and gifts. From award-winning children's titles, best-selling cookbooks, and eclectic pop culture to acclaimed works of art and design, stationery, and journals, we craft publishing that's instantly recognizable for its spirit and creativity. Enjoy our publishing and become part of our community at www.chroniclebooks.com.